Dog Heroes

A STORY POSTER BOOK

with Tales of Dramatic RESCUES,
Courageous JOURNEYS,
and True-Blue FRIENDSHIPS

BY KARL MEYER

Introduction

Dogs do wonderful things. They make us laugh and feel safe. They snatch Frisbees from the air and beg to do it again and again. They wag their tails when we come home and warm us on the couch. They go with us everywhere and never complain. They become part of our family. We become the leaders of their "pack."

In the face of danger, ordinary dogs sometimes become true heroes. There is something in the heart of a dog that makes him or her able to act bravely, just on instinct, and know what to do to save the day. There are stories of dogs who followed their noses to find lost children, and others who rescued entire towns. Some have led their families out of deadly fires, while others have saved drowning sailors.

These heroic hounds can be mutts of no particular type, adopted from animal shelters, or they can be special **breeds** (particular types), carefully trained for a job. Working dogs train for years learning to search, help, and rescue. They search for people in snowslides and collapsed buildings. Some protect soldiers from peril in the lonely places of war, and others locate families lost in earthquakes and storms.

In quieter ways, dogs do amazing jobs for people every day. Guide dogs help blind people get where they need to go. Hearing dogs assist deaf people with their daily lives. Service dogs open doors for people in wheelchairs. They carry packages and fetch medications. Therapy dogs bring warmth and hugs to people who are ill or can't go out.

Here are some of their stories.

Sea Star

England's most famous lifeguard is a dog. Bilbo, a big, friendly Newfoundland weighing more than 100 pounds, takes his job seriously. He passed some of the same rescue tests humans take to become official lifeguards. Bilbo goes on beach patrol with his handler, Steve Jamieson, and visits schools to teach kids about beach safety. There's even a book about him. (In the photo, Bilbo is wearing binoculars just for fun. Human lifeguards use them to spot people who swim far from shore.)

OFFSHORE RESCUE

Thanks to their warm, thick fur, Newfoundlands don't mind cold water, and the **webbing** (extra skin) between their toes helps them swim. Bilbo became famous when his story appeared on TV. He tried to keep a young woman from

Bilbo on duty.

going into the water because the current was dangerous. He stood between her and the beach and wouldn't move, but she went past him anyway into the ocean. When she was nearing dangerous water, he swam out and kept nudging her back inside the safety flags.

That beach has become more popular since Bilbo started working. Maybe more people go there now because they feel safer with Bilbo around!

EXPLORER DOG

Seaman, another Newfoundland, went with explorers Lewis and Clark on their expedition to the Pacific Northwest in 1805. Captain Lewis's dog patrolled the explorers' camps and kept away grizzly bears and buffalo.

Snow Angel

This avalanche search-and-rescue dog is peering into a snow cave in the **Highlands of Scotland.** Thousands of avalanches occur around the world each year. Most happen when no one is around, but sometimes, without warning, great waves of snow can come down a hillside full of skiers or snowmobilers. People can sometimes move aside or get lucky and tumble to the top of the snow, but if they get buried, it's serious. An avalanche can be 10 feet deep and as big as 20 football fields! Because dogs have good noses and are strong diggers, they are very good at finding people buried in the snow.

SNIFF-AND-SEEK

Avalanche dogs train with their handlers for several months to locate people in snow. They learn by playing hide-and-seek burying games that get harder and harder. Dogs' noses are hundreds of times more sensitive than humans' are, and dogs recognize new and different scents immediately. One avalanche dog can search an area the size of a football field in less than 30 minutes. It would take 20 people four hours to search that much snow. The dog will zigzag across a snowy field, sniffing for "pools" of scent. Some dogs have found objects buried under 30 feet of snow!

GOTCHA!

If an avalanche dog finds a person's scent, he stops, sticks his nose in the snow, and begins digging. Then handlers and emergency crews take over the rescue, bringing shovels, warm blankets, and first aid for the victim.

poster photo © Tom Kidd/Alamy • *Dog Heroes, A Story Poster Book,* Storey Publishing

Circle of Pride

Brothers Kennedy, Felix, and Collins live in a crowded compound (fenced-in neighborhood) outside the city of Nairobi, Kenya, in Africa. They are patting an amazing dog named Mkombozi, which means Savior. Mkombozi is a true hero to these brothers, and to other people in the compound.

FINDING FRIENDS

Mkombozi was a **stray** (homeless) dog who came to live with the brothers. There wasn't much food for Mkombozi in the compound, so she had to find it on her own. One day she left the compound to search in a park called the Ngong Forests for scraps to feed her pups. Suddenly she heard a baby cry. It was an infant, a tiny baby left alone in the park.

Mkombozi sensed that the baby was in danger, and she understood what to do. She gently lifted the bag the infant was in and carried the baby from the forest. She crossed a highway and then climbed through a barbed-wire fence to bring the baby back to the safety of the compound.

A HERO AT HOME

In some Nairobi compounds, families of up to 20 people live in mud houses without running water. A compound can be a hard place to live in, but having a dog like Mkombozi can make life a little easier. Our dogs can make us feel lucky and safe. When we're sick or angry or lonely, they cheer us up and make us feel loved.

poster photo © AP IMAGES/Sayyid Azim • *Dog Heroes, A Story Poster Book*, Storey Publishing

Seeing Spots

● ●

Everyone can recognize a Dalmatian, the dog with spots. Dalmatians first came from Europe, where they helped drivers guard their coaches. They stayed calm while working near horses. When they came to the United States, they were trained to race ahead of horse-pulled fire wagons and keep away other dogs that might scare the horses. Even today, Dalmatians are still firehouse **mascots** (symbols).

Can you find the Dalmatian guarding this coach in the 1800s?

DOCTOR'S HELPER

There are amazing stories about Dalmatians. One Dalmatian hero was a dog named Trudi. Thirty years ago, a young woman in England named Gill Lacey noticed that Trudi kept sniffing a spot on Gill's leg. Trudi wouldn't stop. Finally, Gill went to a doctor, who said the spot was a very serious type of cancer. The doctor removed the spot and saved Gill's life. Today, dogs are being trained to help discover early cancers.

JUMPING IN

Sophie was a Dalmatian who lived in Scotland. Although she was deaf, she kept a careful eye on people around her. One early-spring day, when she was only six months old, she saw a five-year-old girl named Georgia Peck stumble and fall into a river. She was swept away. Sophie charged into the water and swam out to where the little girl could grab her paw. Then Sophie paddled little Georgia safely to shore.

poster photo © Gabe Palmer/Alamy; illustration this page © DK Images • *Dog Heroes, A Story Poster Book*, Storey Publishing

Travel Guide

This guide dog has a very important job to do. She has to be alert. She can't be distracted by crowds or afraid of trucks. Guide dogs help blind people cross busy streets and board planes in a world they can't see. Not all dogs can do it. Golden Retrievers, Labrador Retrievers, and German Shepherds make good guide dogs.

SCHOOL LIFE

Before becoming guide dogs, these dogs lead regular puppy lives. They live with families and learn about people. After a year, they are tested at guide dog schools. If they are smart, enjoy learning, and can concentrate and remember things, they may stay at school. Training takes months of hard work. Dogs who graduate are matched with specially selected blind handlers. They must become friends and learn to help each other. Then they can head home together.

TEAMMATES

Together, a guide dog and her handler are truly a team. The handler holds the **harness** (special collar) firmly, so that he can feel when the dog stops at a curb. The handler can also pull on the harness to let the dog know when he wants to slow down, turn right, or speak with someone. In special cases, when a dog sees danger, she knows to stop and disobey, to warn her handler.

When her harness is on, a guide dog is working. She won't stop to be patted. When the harness is off, handlers and dogs get to rest and play.

poster photo © altrendo images/Getty Images • *Dog Heroes, A Story Poster Book*, Storey Publishing

Tough and Loving

Bulldogs are tough-looking canines (dogs) with their strong shoulders, necks, and legs. Their short noses and the folds of skin on their faces make them look like they're frowning, even when they're happy. Don't let their appearance fool you. Most bulldogs are very friendly and lovable.

BOLD SPIRIT

Although bulldogs are sweet and friendly, they are still seen as examples of toughness because they will hold on to something with their teeth and not let go. In England, where this breed began, the bulldog became a symbol of courage during that country's two great wars against Germany. People said, "We're like the bulldog — we don't give up. We will fight on." This stubby dog helped lift the English people's tired spirits when it seemed as though the wars would never end. That "bulldog spirit" helped the English finally win!

Winston Churchill, the prime minister of Great Britain during the great wars, was often compared to a bulldog. Like a bulldog, he was tough and courageous and wouldn't give up. Many Europeans name their bulldogs Churchill as a tribute to the great leader.

GENTLE HEART

Today, gentle bulldogs even help people as therapy dogs. The dogs visit hospitals and nursing homes to lift the spirits of people who are sick, alone, or disabled.

Annabelle, an English Bulldog, entertains the residents of a retirement community.

poster photo © Johan de Meester/ardea.com; photo this page © Akron Beacon Journal/MCT/Landov •
Dog Heroes, A Story Poster Book, Storey Publishing

Going Up?

Kasha can ride ski lifts, snowmobiles, even helicopters, and it's no big deal. She began search-and-rescue training at Mt. Bachelor in Oregon with her ski patrol partner, Paul Clark, when she was four months old. As a team, they became very good at patrolling and safety training.

A GOOD SNIFFER IN THE SNOW

Paul and Kasha worked for years to become a certified rescue team. Kasha learned to ignore noisy crowds, the machinery of chairlifts, and all the distractions at Oregon's largest ski area. Along with all that, she had to learn the precise movements that rescue dogs use to search avalanche fields. Kasha had to focus on Paul's directions and then use her keen senses of smell, sight, and hearing to search an area.

ALL CLEAR!

There were two snowslides at Mt. Bachelor when Kasha was on ski patrol. The people caught in those avalanches were lucky and got themselves out, but Kasha still had a very important job to do. She searched back and forth across the avalanche field, using her nose to make sure no one else was buried in the snow.

Kasha has now retired from Mt. Bachelor, but she is always available if there is an emergency near her Oregon home. She loves having a job to do.

poster photo © Paul Clark, Black and Red Photography • *Dog Heroes, A Story Poster Book*, Storey Publishing

Herd the News?

This Border Collie means business and the sheep know it. He is making them turn where he wants them to go. A Border Collie can control a whole flock with his energy, speed, and brains, but it takes work and training to do his job well. A Border Collie trains for months to learn to wait for his handler's commands and respond instantly. He learns exactly where to stand behind the flock to get the animals to move. With a crouch and a fierce stare, he can make the flock move as if it were his own personal army.

A BREED IS BORN

Border Collies are descended from collies who herded in Great Britain more than 100 years ago. At that time, most collies bit at the heels of sheep and charged them to make them move. This upset the sheep and made them take longer. Farmers noticed that a special collie named Hemp had a different way of herding sheep. He moved sheep calmly, just by crouching and staring into their eyes. Old Hemp became a favorite among farmers and was the father of many pups. He started today's working Border Collie breed. He's every Border Collie's great-great-great-granddad!

A PERFECT HERDER

Border Collies must run quickly, change direction instantly, and work tirelessly. A good Border Collie never takes his eyes off his flock and is able to swiftly bring it to his handler's feet.

Leader of the Pack

Sled dogs are thick-furred, rugged, and full of energy. For thousands of years, they have hauled supplies and pulled home caribou and seal meat for hunting families who live near the North Pole.

SLED DOGS SAVE A TOWN

In January 1925, a deadly disease called diphtheria was sweeping through remote, snowbound Nome, Alaska. Doctors knew that without special **serum** (medicine), children and families would die. But the serum was 1,000 miles away, and the only plane that could deliver it had broken down. The medicine traveled partway by train, but it still had to go another 675 miles through snow and over mountains.

Twenty sled-dog teams raced toward Nome. One team went as far as it could and then handed the medicine to another team farther down the trail. The wind howled and the temperature dropped to 50 degrees below zero. The last team to carry the serum was led by Balto, an Alaskan Malamute. Balto saved his team by keeping them on the trail during a blizzard, when it was nearly impossible to see anything in front of him. On February 2, 1925, he led his team into Nome, bringing the serum that saved the town.

Balto with his partner, Gunnar Kassen.

BALTO'S MONUMENT

Balto became a hero known around the world. A statue of him stands in New York City's Central Park.

poster photo © AP IMAGES/Robert F. Bukaty; photo this page courtesy the Cleveland Public Library Photograph Collection • *Dog Heroes, A Story Poster Book,* Storey Publishing

Backyard Hero

Ordinary dogs with no training do amazing things for people all the time. Some people say they help because they are smart or brave. Others say dogs help because they see people as part of their **pack** (their dog family). However it works, wonderful things happen when dogs and people are together.

BARKING THE ALARM

Boston Terriers, like the one in this photo, are bouncy, bright, and friendly. They like games and sometimes they bark a lot. Whitney and Brook Lovatt live near the ocean in Stuart, Florida. Their Boston Terrier, Tyson, likes to play with his toys and keep an eye on things around the house.

One warm day Whitney's sister Amy was visiting with her 10-month-old son, Lios. The TV was on and the patio doors were open. Brook Lovatt heard a splash. Like everyone else, when it's warm, Tyson likes to cool off, so Brook thought Tyson had tossed his toy in the pool again. But Tyson started barking and kept barking. Brook got up to investigate, then ran when he saw Lios facedown in the water. Brook is a boat captain, so he knew what to do to help Lios breathe. Someone called 911 and soon an ambulance arrived.

A MIRACULOUS SAVE

With Brook's help, Lios started breathing. Later, at the hospital, they said Lios would be fine, saved by Tyson's bark and a quick-thinking uncle.

Lion Heart

Chow Chows are known for their thick fur, which looks almost like the mane of a lion, and their purple tongues. They are also known for their funny way of walking. They keep their back legs fairly stiff and walk with small, quick steps. Chow Chows come from China, where ancient palaces still have stone figures of small, lionlike guardians standing outside. Some people believe these sculptures honor the loyal, lion hearts of Chow Chows from long ago.

This "Fu Dog," a statue of a Chinese lion that resembles a dog, stands guard in Beijing.

BRAVE PROTECTORS

Chow Chows are strong and loyal, and work to protect their people. One woman's Chow Chow even lost his life when he jumped in front of an alligator in a Florida river to save his owner. The woman had been playing catch with her dog when she decided to cool off by diving from her dock into the river. An alligator shot across the water almost instantly. Amazingly, the Chow Chow jumped between them, enabling her to swim to safety.

AN ANCIENT BREED

The Chow Chow is one of the oldest breeds. The first Chow Chows were born thousands of years ago, descended from wolves that lived in ancient Asia. They were used as guard dogs in their homeland of China for hundreds of years. One emperor kept 2,500 pairs of Chow Chows!

poster photo © Cheryl A. Artelt; photo this page © DK Images • *Dog Heroes, A Story Poster Book*, Storey Publishing

Loki to the Rescue

Loki is demonstrating his rescue training. Loki and his handler Roger Matthews are members of the Colorado Task Force 1 Urban Search and Rescue team. They were heroes to two hikers who had been lost for five days near Rocky Mountain National Park. The pilot of a search plane first saw the hikers and radioed to the rescue team for help. Loki picked up the scent of the hikers in the air and led Roger to them.

INTO THE TOUGH SPOTS

Search dogs play a key role in locating missing people after disasters like hurricanes and earthquakes. Some rescue workers like to use specific breeds, but mutts from animal shelters can make excellent search dogs, too. When planes crashed into the World Trade Center, hundreds of search dog teams arrived. There were many different types of dogs, such as Black and Yellow Labrador Retrievers, German Shepherds, Golden Retrievers, collies, and mutts.

DOCS FOR DOGS

Like the firefighters, police, doctors, nurses, and volunteers, those dogs got bruised, injured, and exhausted during long days of searching. But handlers kept praising the dogs for their efforts, and in return the dogs helped cheer up tired rescuers. So many rescue dogs helped at the World Trade Center disaster that **veterinarians** (animal doctors) set up minihospitals to sew up their injuries and give them water.

Dogs with Drive

This cowgirl hasn't found a lost pup. She is bringing her tired partner home after a day of training. This Australian Cattle Dog pup may be worn out from learning commands from her handler. Cattle dogs are smart and independent. They need to be trained each day to remind them that the handler is the "big dog." When this pup is older, she'll gather flocks of sheep or drive dozens of cattle to exactly where her master wants them.

BORN TO HERD

Australian Cattle Dogs love to work. They were born to herd, guard, and run in the dry **outback** (countryside) of Australia. The first cattle dogs were offspring of collies and **dingoes** (Australia's wild dogs). Collies were natural herders and dingoes were tough hunters. Their pups, the cattle dogs, were smart and strong and could work all day driving cattle.

This Australian Cattle Dog is showing how he got the nickname Heeler.

Because they have a lot of energy, Australian Cattle Dogs need plenty of exercise. They get bored if they don't have work to do. They are in love with their jobs and are just waiting for that next steer to stray!

WHAT'S IN A NICKNAME?

Australian Cattle Dogs get cattle to move by biting at their hind legs. Their natural heel-nipping instinct helped give them another name: Heeler.

✚ Just Dropping In

Search-and-rescue dogs do dangerous work. This Golden Retriever and his partner are training in Germany. They may be practicing to go into a collapsed building or to be lowered into a place where a fire has been. They will train for many months before they have a real assignment.

DISASTER HELP

Search-and-rescue dogs help find people who are lost or injured after fires, earthquakes, hurricanes, floods, and other disasters. Not just any dog can be a search-and-rescue dog. He must be smart and energetic and have an excellent nose. He also must be eager to learn and have a hunting instinct that makes him enjoy finding things.

There are two basic types of search-and-rescue dogs: **trailing dogs** and **air-scent dogs.** Trailing dogs focus on the scent of a single person, following that one smell and moving close to the ground. Air-scent dogs sniff the air for clues. If they smell a new human scent in a rescue area, they eagerly lead the search team to the lost person.

ARSON DOGS

More like detectives than rescuers, **arson dogs** are experts at finding the exact spot where a fire started. Some can sniff out chemicals to help prove a fire has been started on purpose. Labrador Retrievers make excellent arson dogs because they are good at identifying scents, and they are outgoing and easy to work with.

All Smiles

This young man and the little guy he's holding are clearly enjoying each other's company. Dogs make people feel happy. Scenes like this happen in thousands of places every day. Sometimes it's the neighborhood mutt, just wagging his tail, bringing joy to his friends. At other times it's a specially trained therapy dog who cheers up a person in a hospital or nursing home. These dogs are chosen for their ability to bring warmth, friendship, and a smile to people who are unable to go outside or to walk on their own.

HEALING VISITS

Therapy dogs visit any place where they might help people feel better. They go to hospitals, nursing homes, and camps for kids who are very ill. Therapy dogs are special pets, not a special breed, but not all dogs can become therapy dogs. They must be gentle, happy to meet strangers, and patient about being petted or cuddled by many people.

THE FIRST THERAPY DOGS

A nurse named Elaine Smith trained the first therapy dogs in the United States. She'd worked in hospitals in Europe and saw that a visiting dog made patients feel happier and calmer. Dogs even seemed to help them get well faster. She started a program called Therapy Dogs International, Inc., that has trained many of these visitors and their handlers. Today, therapy dogs make thousands of people happy with their visits.

Protecting Our Troops

This military dog is catching a ride on a tank that has been painted tan to blend in with the desert around it. Each day, hundreds of military working dogs and their soldier handlers guard the borders of countries around the world. Soldiers who work in countries at war have dangerous jobs. Trained German Shepherds, Dobermans, and other dogs help keep them safe. They hear, see, and smell things that soldiers can't. The dogs signal when an enemy is near, and they sniff out exploding traps so the soldiers don't step on them. They also find injured soldiers and bring them medicine.

A HISTORY OF HELPING

Dogs have protected soldiers for hundreds of years. Four thousand dogs helped soldiers during the Vietnam War. A German Shepherd named Bruiser warned soldiers there was going to be a surprise attack. When his handler was injured, Bruiser dragged him to safety. Another dog, Mac, saved his handler from a poisonous snake by letting the snake bite him instead. Both Mac and Bruiser were hurt, but they survived, and the soldiers called them heroes.

A British soldier removes a message from a dog courier during World War I.

HEROES' HONORS

Stubby, a famous terrier, helped American soldiers fighting in France during World War I. Stubby traveled to dangerous places and lived with soldiers in the field. He helped on patrols, and once he even discovered a German spy. Stubby crept up on the man and held him by the pants until soldiers captured him. Stubby's companionship and loyalty helped cheer up the troops. When the war ended, Stubby was honored with six medals for his bravery.

poster photo © Stocktrek Images/Alamy; photo this page © The Art Archive/Culver Pictures •
Dog Heroes, A Story Poster Book, Storey Publishing

Trail Blazer

There are many true stories about heroic St. Bernards, big mountain dogs who come from Switzerland. They are famous for rescuing travelers caught in the snows at the Great St. Bernard Pass, high in the Swiss Alps. Before cars and roads came along, there was just a narrow path across those mountains. The weather could be very bad, making travel along the path treacherous.

LEADING THE WAY

Hundreds of years ago, monks ran a **hospice** (free hotel) at the top of the pass to warm and feed those who made the dangerous journey. The monks searched for lost travelers and guided others down the mountain. St. Bernard dogs walked with the monks and travelers through the pass. The dogs' deep chests helped them push through the snow. Their good noses and hearing helped them guide people safely through blizzards and fog, saving hundreds of lives.

Monks from the Great St. Bernard Pass play with their dogs.

BARRY'S RESCUES

The monks began training St. Bernards to guide and search on their own. The dogs could find people who were nearly frozen in the snow. Some dogs would stay to warm the people by lying next to them, while other dogs would go back for help. The most famous rescuer was Barry. This bold mountain dog went out on the worst snowy nights to help lost travelers. Barry rescued more than 40 people. After he died, in 1814, his body was put on display, and it can still be seen today in a museum in Bern, Switzerland.

An Unlikely Hero

This is Jake, and he's a hero to many people. But before he became a hero, Jake had to be rescued himself. He was a pup living on the streets before his handler, Mary Flood, adopted him. He had a broken leg and a bad hip, but Mary and Jake liked each other instantly. Mary took Jake for surgery, and after a while Jake was healed. Mary is a rescue worker, and she trained Jake to help in water, snow, and other emergency rescues. He was a natural.

SAVING THE DAY

Jake went with Mary on dozens of missions, in places where hundreds of people had been injured. The partners worked hard to locate victims after Hurricanes Rita and Katrina. When the World Trade Center's Twin Towers fell, Mary Flood and Jake were there, too. For 17 days, Jake searched for missing people, crawling into dangerous, smoky places too small for humans. He became a favorite with some of the rescue workers. When they were feeling very tired, Jake would drop his ball in front of them, reminding them he could still play. Jake cheered them up and helped them keep going.

LONG LIFE AS A HELPER

When Jake got too old for rescue work, he still liked to help. He helped teach other dogs how to search for people, and he visited sick people in hospitals. Jake lived to be 12 years old. That's old for a Lab, even one who is a hero.

poster photo © AP IMAGES/Steve C. Wilson • *Dog Heroes, A Story Poster Book,* Storey Publishing

Furry Life Saver

This dog is going to school in Italy and learning how to jump from a helicopter to save people. He will learn to plunge into chilly lakes and choppy seas from a hovering helicopter. Once in the water, he will swim powerfully, helping keep people afloat until they can be pulled in.

HELICOPTER HEROES

Dogs from all over the world attend Ferrucio Pilenga's Italian School of Dog Rescue to learn water rescue. Water dogs have helped people for centuries, towing boats, pulling in fishing nets, and retrieving ducks for hunters, but it takes special training to learn how to jump from a helicopter. Signor Pilenga's first student was his own Newfoundland, named Mas. With hard work and some help from the Italian navy, he trained Mas to rescue people in water. Always working with a human partner, Mas learned to swim with a rope to a drowning person and to pull a life raft full of people through rough seas.

WATER SAVIORS

Rescue dogs must be big, with thick fur, and love water. Newfoundlands and Labrador Retrievers are good choices, but other types do great work, too. In 1925, a famous Siberian Husky named Togo jumped into freezing water in Alaska to help pull a sled loaded with medicine back across a dangerous break in the ice.

poster photo © REUTERS/Alessandro Garofalo/Landov • *Dog Heroes, A Story Poster Book,* Storey Publishing

Small Body, Big Heart

Midge, a Chihuahua from Ohio, is wearing her police vest. When Midge was just three months old, her handler, Sheriff Dan McClelland, took one look at this smart little **canine** (dog) and said, "She could be a police dog." So, at three months, Midge began training for police work. She trained to be a sniffer dog who could find drugs in tight places, like the trunks of small cars, that big dogs couldn't. She also had a very good nose for finding things that smelled unusual, and she was naturally curious. It took months of training, but this little lion joined the big dogs of Geauga County's K-9 Unit in 2006.

Midge with her handler, Sheriff Dan McClelland.

MINIROYALTY

Chihuahuas are the world's smallest dogs, but they don't seem to know it. They are smart, quick, and brave, protecting their owners the way lions guard their families. Chihuahuas seem to have no idea they weigh just 4 to 6 pounds. These tiny dogs from Mexico have always been cherished for their size. They have been companion dogs for hundreds of years and once were part of royal ceremonies.

LOST AND FOUND!

When invading armies defeated Mexico's ancient kingdoms, these dogs nearly disappeared, too. But in 1850, a small group of Chihuahuas was found near Mexican ruins. Slowly, people rediscovered this breed, and it became popular once again.

Guardian Pup

Maybe this Great Pyrenees pup doesn't realize that he is smaller than the sheep he's learning to guard. We all start out small, and our confidence grows as we get bigger. This pup will grow and learn to guard bigger flocks of sheep and lambs. He'll keep them safe from coyotes, dogs, cougars, and bears. This little guy has a big job ahead.

PALACE GUARD

Great Pyrenees have been guarding flocks of sheep for centuries. They first protected sheep from wolves and bears in the mountain pastures of France and Spain. Later, they guarded the palaces of kings. In 1675, King Louis XIV of France declared the thick-furred Great Pyrenees "the Royal Dog of France." These dogs still guard flocks and watch over homes in many countries.

FIRE ESCAPE

A dog named Kodiak was guarding sheep in Carnation, Washington, one night when his owners heard the roar of their barn burning. Their sheep, dogs, and cats were in that barn. They ran to help, but the flames were huge. They couldn't go close to the barn, and it burned to the ground. They were heartbroken, thinking that all of their animals were lost. But then a fireman said that he'd seen a big white dog. It was Kodiak, their Great Pyrenees. He'd saved the animals, getting burns on his legs while leading them to safety. His owner cried when she saw Kodiak. He was a part of their family, and she was so happy that he was safe.

poster photo © Cat Urbigkit • *Dog Heroes, A Story Poster Book,* Storey Publishing

Hope and Heroism

This decorated dog is Endal, a famous Yellow Lab service dog. He is wearing the PDSA Gold Medal, an important British award given to very brave, loyal animals. Endal is a hero to his handler, Allen Parton, a war veteran from the United Kingdom. Officer Parton was injured during the Gulf War; he couldn't walk any more and had trouble remembering things. At times he couldn't speak. He was very unhappy. Then he was introduced to Endal and he began to enjoy life again.

HANDY HELPER

Endal helps Allen in amazing ways. Endal can load laundry, shop, and even use a bank machine. When Allen couldn't talk, Endal learned dozens of signals so he could help his handler with the things he needed.

In 2001, a car knocked Allen out of his wheelchair. Nobody on the street stopped. Endal turned him over, grabbed a blanket, and covered him. He got out Allen's cell phone for him and then ran for help. Endal became a celebrity on TV and in the news. He was filmed many times. Today, Endal and Allen Parton teach people about the importance of service dogs.

SENSATIONAL SERVICE DOGS

Guide dogs and hearing dogs assist people who can't see or hear. Other service dogs like Endal, also called **assistance dogs,** help people walk, open doors, fetch clothes, or get medications and turn on lights. Some can even signal for help. Most service dogs wear a **harness** (a special collar), but some don't, so you can't always tell if a dog is a service dog.

The Collie Club

Collies are known for being very loyal pets. In 1938, Eric Knight wrote a famous story called "Lassie Come Home," about a friendship between a boy and his collie, Lassie. In this **fictional** (made-up) story, Lassie is taken many miles away but heroically makes her way back to her dear friend. Readers loved it so much that new stories about Lassie the dog hero were made into Hollywood movies, TV shows, and dozens of books.

TV star Lassie with her best friend, Timmy, photographed in the 1960s.

A REAL-LIFE LIFESAVER

Collies also do great things in real life. In 2008, a two-and-a-half-year-old Canadian girl named Destiny wandered off into the woods near her aunt's farm. Too young to know danger, Destiny was just looking for her dad. The grown-ups quickly discovered that she was gone and called the police. Shilo, her aunt's collie, was gone too.

Rescue teams searched through the night for the missing child. Just as the sun began to come out the next morning, police received a call that Destiny had been found, with just a few scratches. Shilo had saved her. The collie had lain at her side, keeping her warm through the chilly night.

CHOSEN BY A QUEEN

Collies first came from Great Britain, where they helped farmers herd sheep. But they also made good pets. In the mid-1800s, England's Queen Victoria noticed this and decided to keep her own collies. Queen Victoria made the collie breed famous.

poster photo © Petra Wegner/Alamy; photo this page © CBS Photo Archive/Getty Images • *Dog Heroes, A Story Poster Book,* Storey Publishing

The Nosiest Dogs

Bloodhounds live to smell. The folds of skin and fur on their faces help them trap scents. Their sense of smell can be 100 times better than that of a human, and they can even detect a tiny drop of blood in a bucket of water. The first world-famous bloodhound was named Pluto, and he belonged to Mickey Mouse. Pluto's first job as a cartoon hound was to track prisoners.

PARTNERS IN SOLVING CRIME

Nick Carter was a real-life bloodhound from Kentucky. He worked with his human partner, Captain G. V. Mullikin, to help track and arrest more than 600 suspects. Nick would sniff something that only the suspect had touched, like a piece of clothing or a pillow. He'd memorize that person's scent and lead Captain Mullikin to where the suspect was. Once, Nick followed the trail of a suspect for four days until he found him! Bloodhounds also help find people of all ages who are lost.

A FAMOUS CAPTURE

For hundreds of years, bloodhounds have helped hunters follow the trails of animals. But bloodhounds have also helped capture real villains. In April 1977, James Earl Ray, the man who shot Dr. Martin Luther King Jr., escaped from jail in Tennessee with five other prisoners. For two days, James Earl Ray ran free. But trained bloodhounds used their noses to find him where he hid in the brush eight miles away. The police took him back to prison.

Japan's Hero

The Akita is Japan's most famous dog breed, known for its strength, loyalty, and courage. Hundreds of years ago, Akitas pulled sleds and guarded families in snowy northern Japan. Emperors kept them to help hunt bear and chase deer. Today, Akita statues honor these dogs' courage and faithfulness. Small statues are given as gifts to celebrate new babies and wish people good health.

EVER FAITHFUL

The most famous Akita was Hachiko. As a puppy, Hachiko began walking with his owner, Professor Ueno, to the Shibuya train station. When the train left, Hachiko would go home, and when the train returned, Hachiko would walk back to the station. For two years, Hachiko met his friend at the station. One evening the dog waited and waited, but the professor did not get off his train. His owner had died suddenly at work.

Hachiko could not understand that his friend would not return. He was given a new home, but he kept running back to his former owner's house. When he didn't find his friend there, he went to the station to wait for Professor Ueno's train to arrive. People recognized Hachiko and they began feeding him. Hachiko stayed and stayed, waiting for his friend. The station became Hachiko's home. He stayed at the station for 10 years, and he died near the place where he waited for his friend each day.

HACHIKO'S MONUMENT

A statue of Hachiko (see photo at right) stands near his waiting spot at the Shibuyu train station.

Watching Over the Herd

Mary Jane is an Australian Cattle Dog. Cattle dogs are herders who help ranchers move cattle and flocks of sheep from place to place on big farms. They stare into the eyes and nip at the heels of stray sheep and cattle until the animals go where they are needed. Cattle dogs are smart, fast, and unafraid of cattle 10 times their size.

A PARTNER ON THE FARM

Dogs' lives are shorter than ours. It can hurt to lose a dog who has been a great friend. Lee O'Dell is a sheep rancher in Idaho. His dog Janie was always with him, helping him move his sheep from pasture to pasture. For nine years she helped Lee keep his herd safe, running off coyotes and helping find strays. Janie worked in rain and snow and heat. She loved riding next to Lee in his pickup truck. When Janie died suddenly, Lee and his wife were heartbroken.

A HEALING HEART

But they still needed help with the sheep. The O'Dells looked everywhere for another dog. They finally found a special puppy who was bright and alert. They brought her home and named her Mary Jane in honor of Janie. Lee began to train her. The young dog loved her new home and herding chores. Today, Mary Jane rides with Lee in his truck. "She brings great joy to my wife and me," Lee says.

A K-9 Team

Police dogs do police jobs. They search buildings, chase suspects, and sniff out drugs, guns, and explosives. They must be smart, well trained, and unafraid of people in dangerous situations. They must also have excellent noses and obey only orders given by their handlers. Police dogs and their handlers are a team. Officers and their dogs work together and even live together. They never stop practicing their police skills.

BRAVERY ON THE JOB

Police work can be dangerous. That's why it's so important to carefully train a **K-9** (dog) team. Most police dogs are German Shepherds. They are fast, strong, and aggressive. Sometimes just seeing a police dog will scare suspects into surrendering, but if they run, these dogs are trained to capture people. They hold the suspects with their strong jaws and won't let go until their handlers arrive.

CAPTURING A SUSPECT

Suspicious fires damaged many homes in Palm Bay, Florida, in 2008. A young man saw someone throw a burning object from a car and start a fire. The young man's mother phoned 911. Police spotted the suspect's car, but the driver ran off. Sixty officers and a helicopter searched, but it was a police dog who found the suspect hidden in tall grass. Police officers arrested the suspect.

poster photo © AP IMAGES/Amy Sancetta • *Dog Heroes, A Story Poster Book,* Storey Publishing

High-Altitude Hero

This eager Golden Retriever is part of an avalanche search-and-rescue team. Golden Retrievers think that rescue training is a game. They practice finding victims hidden in snow, hoping to be rewarded with a game of tug-of-war with their handlers at the end. Golden Retrievers first came from Scotland, where they helped hunters fetch ducks that had been shot over water. Retrievers love fetching and they love water. They are also loyal, playful, and trainable. These traits are what make them great avalanche dogs.

EVERY MINUTE COUNTS

Thousands of real avalanches take place around the world each year. Luckily, most happen when no one is around. But sometimes people do get caught beneath these thundering snowslides. This is when avalanche rescue dogs go into action. They are so good at sniffing for hints of buried people that they can work as fast as 20 human searchers. This is necessary in a real rescue, because people need to be found within 30 minutes of the avalanche.

DOC SAVES THE DAY

When Jeff Eckland was caught in an avalanche in Nevada in 1993, he was buried deep in snow. He couldn't move and had broken bones. Jeff knew he didn't have much time. He also knew that Doc, a trained avalanche dog, was nearby. He waited, but it got harder to breathe. Then he heard voices and felt a rush of fresh air. Doc, the Golden Retriever, had dug in and found him. Jeff was going to live.

poster photo © Paul Clark, Black and Red Photography • *Dog Heroes, A Story Poster Book*, Storey Publishing

Great Guardian

Khan is a Doberman Pinscher. These dogs are strong, alert, and loyal, and they like to work. The first Dobermans were given important jobs like protecting people and guarding places. Now many people keep Dobermans because they like to have them with the family. Even at home, Dobermans like Khan take their guard jobs seriously.

A SAVING ANGEL

Khan was a rescued dog. His owner didn't take care of him. Hurt and hungry, Khan was taken away from his owner and nursed back to health. He went to live with a new family, the Svilicics, in Australia. He was happy to have a new family and a new home. He liked to keep watch over 17-month-old Charlotte while she played in the yard.

One day, Khan started to behave very strangely when Charlotte was playing. He acted nervous and began to shove the little girl as if he was trying to move her. Suddenly he grabbed Charlotte by her diaper, tossed her aside, and barked loudly. Charlotte had been playing near a poisonous brown snake that was about to bite her.

Khan saved Charlotte, but the snake bit him. Luckily, help was near. A **veterinarian** (animal doctor) gave Khan a shot that saved his life.

GOOD WORKERS

Because Doberman Pinschers are very alert and energetic, they are often trained to be military and police dogs.

All in a Day's Work

Tucker, a Labrador Retriever, practices search and rescue with his partner, Paul Molnar, every day. He is trained not to let the noise of helicopters or the excitement of busy ski slopes distract him. In an avalanche, he must be all business. He can search a snowy field eight times faster than humans can. This might save a skier's life.

LOVABLE AND HEROIC

Labrador Retrievers are the most popular dogs in America. They are friendly, helpful, intelligent, and easy to train. They seem to be good at everything. In the past, they retrieved ducks for hunters and hauled nets for fishermen. Today, they search snowslides, find survivors in collapsed buildings, and sniff out drugs and explosives. Labs are also the number one breed of guide dog.

FAITHFUL FRIEND

Some Labs are just special. Dorado was with his blind owner, Omar Rivera, on the 71st floor of the World Trade Center when the planes crashed into the towers. Omar thought he would not escape alive. He unhooked Dorado from his **harness** (special collar), hoping at least his dog could get out. People rushed past as glass broke around them. Omar made his way to the stairs. Suddenly, he felt a familiar push at his knee. It was the steady, guiding shoulder of Dorado, who had come back to find his owner. With Dorado leading on one side and a friend on the other, Omar escaped to safety down 70 flights of stairs.

Resources

Books about Heroic Dogs

Balto and the Great Race
by Elizabeth Cody Kimmel
This book teaches about sled racing and the most
famous sled racer, Balto.

Bilbo Says
This book tells the story of Bilbo the canine
lifeguard; available online at *www.bilbosays.com*.

The Bravest Dog Ever: The True Story of Balto
by Natalie Standiford
A beginning reader's book about the brave sled
dog Balto, it has an accompanying CD with
music and sound effects.

Dogs with Jobs
by Kim Kachanoff and Merrily Weisbord
This is a collection of profiles of real dogs from
around the world who have extraordinary jobs.

Hachiko: The True Story of a Loyal Dog
by Pamela S. Turner and Yan Nascimbene
A small, square picture book, this is about the
famous Japanese dog Hachiko.

Hachiko Waits
by Leslea Newman
This is a fictionalized account of the true story of
the legendary Japanese dog.

Lad: A Dog
by Albert Payson Terhune
This collection of very popular magazine stories
centers on an amazing collie named Lad.

Lassie Come Home
by Eric Knight
The original story of the amazing collie who
battles all odds to find her companion Joe.

Organizations to Know About

American Rescue Dog Association (ARDA)
www.ardainc.org
ARDA organizes volunteer search-and-rescue
teams across the United States to assist police
agencies and other organizations in finding
missing persons.

**American Society for the Prevention of Cruelty
to Animals (ASPCA)**
www.aspca.org
Founded in 1866, the ASPCA fights against
injustice and cruelty to animals.

The Humane Society of the United States
www.hsus.org
The nation's largest animal protection agency, the
Humane Society calls itself a voice for animals.

**National Association for Search and Rescue
(NASR)** *www.nasar.org*
The NASR trains humans and their canine
partners to search for and rescue people who are
lost or stranded.

Therapy Dogs International, Inc.
www.tdi-dog.org
Founded by Elaine Smith, Therapy Dogs
International tests and registers therapy dogs,
who visit hospitals, nursing homes, and any
other place they are needed.

The United States War Dogs Association, Inc.
www.uswardogs.org
A nonprofit organization, it promotes the long
history of military service dogs.

The mission of Storey Publishing is to serve our customers by publishing practical information that encourages personal independence in harmony with the environment.

Edited by Sarah Guare and Deborah Burns
Art direction and book design by Jessica Armstrong

Cover photograph by © Paul Clark, Black and Red Photography
Additional interior photographs by © Jochen Tack/Alamy, title page;
© Ron Kimball/www.kimballstock.com, intro page;
© Greg Ruffing/Redux, this page

Special thanks to Xavier Vilaubi, Dani and Matt Gulino, and Ben and Sam Greeman
for reviewing the photographs in this book.

For additional information, please contact Storey Publishing, 210 MASS MoCA Way, North Adams, MA 01247.
Storey books are available for special premium and promotional uses and for customized editions.
For further information, please call 1-800-793-9396.

Printed in Hong Kong by Elegance
10 9 8 7 6 5 4 3 2 1